IT'S (NOT) THE THOUGHT THAT COUNTS

IT'S (NOT) THE THOUGHT THAT COUNTS

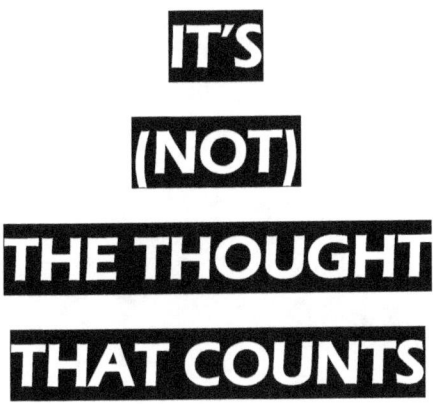

Reflection of a marketer
on selfish altruism

Victoria Schaal

IT'S (NOT) THE THOUGHT THAT COUNTS

Cover by Michele dell'Oman

Copyright © 2024 Victoria Schaal. All rights reserved. No part of this publication may be reproduced, distributed, or transmitted in any form or by any means, including photocopying, recording, or other electronic or mechanical methods, without the prior written permission of the publisher or the author, except in the case of brief quotations embodied in critical reviews and certain other non-commercial uses permitted by copyright law. For permission requests, write to the author, addressed:

vs@victoriaschaal.com

www.victoriaschaal.com

IT'S (NOT) THE THOUGHT THAT COUNTS

*Dedicated to all those
who will take the time
to read this book fully*

IT'S (NOT) THE THOUGHT THAT COUNTS

CONTENTS

Prologue	Page 1
The Battlefield	Page 5
Social What?	Page 10
Whence Altruism?	Page 17
Any Volunteers?	Page 38
War or Peace	Page 47
Selfish Altruism	Page 51
Sharing is Caring	Page 64
The Thoughts That Do Count	Page 77
Bibliography	Page 87
About the Author	Page 93
By the Same Author	Page 98

IT'S (NOT) THE THOUGHT THAT COUNTS

PROLOGUE

The genesis of this text traces back to my late teens, when it originated as an assignment regarding the existence of altruism within social marketers' and non-profit organisations' activities for my marketing module at the University of Exeter's Business School.

Years later, quite serendipitously, I rediscovered this text and reread it. The most astonishing revelation was that my thoughts, initially crafted as those of an overly confident and naïve but smart young student, remained largely unchanged. The period that elapsed between completing the assignment and revisiting it merely served as a confirmation.

Over the years, as I accumulated more experiences in both the business world and volunteering, my original conclusions not only endured but were reinforced. These experiences didn't prompt a revision; instead, they enriched my perspectives with additional knowledge and insights.

The culmination of editing and expanding this text, coupled with the research involved and my personal journey, allowed me to develop a more nuanced understanding of social marketing, non-profit organisations (NPOs) and, on a broader scale, altruism.

As I will acknowledge in the further pages, cynicism has always been inherent in my nature, and this case was no exception. Nevertheless, prior to composing this piece, I confess to harbouring a somewhat superficial opinion.

However, I have come to appreciate that knowledge is paramount in forming astute and balanced judgments. This writing endeavour provided me with the opportunity to gather solid blocks of information in various forms, allowing me to construct a well-informed conclusion. I hope it will do the same for you. Enjoy the read!

IT'S (NOT) THE THOUGHT THAT COUNTS

THE BATTLEFIELD

I like to picture trade as a battlefield. Sellers are the infantry: foot soldiers who engage buyers one by one, commonly armed with persuasive speeches but often carrying heavier weapons like discounts. Marketing, on the other hand, is the artillery that lies back, atop the hill. It drops promotional bombs on large segments of audience in the hope of hitting as many buyers as possible or the powerful generals of big companies and organisations.

The study and making of marketing has proven to be extremely interesting to me since my teens: the relationship between marketing activities and the behaviour of society is a concept as complex as the human mind. People are different and as such, people behave differently. Different people like different things. Different people have different wants. Different people have different needs. Such a fact represents the labyrinthine trenches which sellers and marketers attempt to explore. This maze is the part of marketing that has always attracted me the most, both as an academic study and as a business tool.

However, due to my personal past experiences, which I will use in this reflection to draw examples, I found myself wondering whether there is room for altruism in such a battlefield. Can altruism exist and be part of my profession? We marketers are often heavily criticised and considered *bad guys*, paid off by villain big companies, who lie to get money out of naive consumers, who overcharge poor citizens, who create *fake needs* and so on.

Although I naturally nurture a drastically divergent vision of marketers, I do question us and our practices a great deal.

I thought that investigating the entire concept of altruism and apply my research and reflections to commercial marketing would contribute to clarify marketers' reasons and aims both in my head and in yours. I also thought that the investigation would reach deeper reflections and draw more reliable conclusions if I compared and contrasted the concepts of altruism and self-interest not solely in commercial marketing but especially in social marketing and in organisations that deem to fight egoism, such as NPOs.

IT'S (NOT) THE THOUGHT THAT COUNTS

SOCIAL WHAT?

As a result of the arising of social media as an additional advertising platform, social marketing nowadays is often misidentified, especially amongst the young generation.

Social media and social marketing are two totally different concepts. The former is merely a business tool through which modern marketers are channelling advertising activities, the latter is an entire subsidiary of the mother discipline of marketing. Hence, what is social marketing exactly?

The concept of social marketing was first mentioned in the 1970s by two fathers of the discipline: Kotler and Zaltman[1]. They define it as "the design, implementation, and control of programmes calculated to influence the acceptability of social ideas and involving considerations of product planning, pricing, communication, distribution and marketing research"[2].

Although several definitions exist, the latter is the most commonly used, as well as being the one that Hastings, a pillar in the academic business world,

---

[1] MacFadyen et al, 1999.

[2] Kotler; Zaltman, 1971, Pg.5.

favours[3].

However, Andreasen, another renown scholar, explains that social marketing has evolved in time, starting from being a discipline that attempted to improve individual well-being through the use of marketing theory, to becoming an innovative approach aiming at social change[4]. The study area, thus, expanded over the past decades and the relatively recent environment-driven *green marketing* now falls under the social marketing umbrella too.

Social marketing nowadays deals with big societal issues, for instance the consumption of those nasty

---

[3] Hastings, 2007.

[4] Andreasen, 2003.

demerit goods[5]. Being a smoker myself, I have been exposed to numerous social marketing campaigns attempting to alter my deemed *bad* habit: I have been disgusted by the photos on the packs of cigarettes, I know by heart all the threatening sentences on them, every day I see the adverts on the media that kindly invite me to release myself from this harm. Despite all this, I have not changed my behaviour. Along with the chemically addictive nature of tobacco products, one of the main reasons is that I have always regarded social marketing campaigns with rather cynical eyes. I am aware that social marketers aim at changing the society's harmful habits, but what I can hardly picture is why they care about the well-being of others.

---

[5] Hastings, 2007

Cynicism is also the reason why I am sceptical of NPOs. A non-profit organisation is "one that is precluded, by external regulation or its own governance structure, from distributing its financial surplus to those who control the use of organisational assets"[6]. Although those in charge possess a limited range of ownership rights, like the right to decide where and how the resources are allocated, they are not in the position of generating profit through the use of such resources or from selling their rights[7].

Both social marketing and NPOs seek to benefit people through attempting to influence, discourage and change social behaviours. Yet, there is a key difference between the two: the former is a set of

---

[6] Steinberg; Powell, 2006, Pg.1

[7] Ben-Ner; Jones, 1995

marketing practices which principally targets change in the society as a whole[8]; while the latter is a type of organisation/association that aims at helping specific people in need.

Nevertheless, such a distinction does not prevent NPOs to make use of social marketing as well; hence from the perspective of this text, the two are closely linked[9].

---

[8] Andreasen, 2003 and Steinberg; Powell, 2006

[9] Andreasen, 2001

IT'S (NOT) THE THOUGHT THAT COUNTS

WHENCE ALTRUISM?

Just like with social marketing, I am sceptical regarding the reasons that drive people to engage in NPOs and concern about the others' situations. *Why do they care?!*

In my view, there are only two possible answers to my question: either altruism really exists or it is the opportunity to gain something in return that drives individuals to help the collective. These options have been debated for decades.

Let us start from the very beginning: a little historical bracket.

Altruism was coined by the French philosopher Auguste Compte. Positivist at heart, he is considered to be the father of the discipline of praxeology. He defined *altruisme* as the opposite of egoism[10]. The term derives from the Italian *altrui* which finds its origin in the Latin word *alter* that simply signifies *the others* or *other people*[11].

In economic psychology, altruism is defined as "being an individual behaviour of assistant to others, in its own expenses"[12]; basically it is the act of

---

[10] Compte; Congrev, 1891

[11] Cicloni, 1825

[12] Kapoor, 2013, Pg.315

helping a party with or without being asked, at your own risk and/or cost. In sociological studies too, the purpose of altruistic behaviours is to benefit others, even when this damages the actor[13].

Thus, we can make an educated association between altruism and the concept of *philanthropy*, a Greek term which literally signifies *love for humanity*[14].

The main question at this stage is the following: are social marketers and NPOs altruistic and philanthropic, because they focus on the well-being of others?

---

[13] Monroe, 1996

[14] Zunz, 2012.

Stern, Dietz and Kalof believe that altruism plays a vital role in human behaviour. In fact, in their study, which focuses more specifically on environmental responsibility, the scholars state that both egoism and altruism are forms of influences on an individual's ecological conduct. Furthermore, they draw a distinction between *social* and *bio-spherical* altruism: the former is defined as the genuine concern for the well-being of others, while the latter is the care for non-human elements of the environment[15]. By asserting that altruism has an impact on the human conduct and by elaborating two sub-categories, Stern, Dietz and Kalof clearly express that the concept of altruism definitely exists.

Nonetheless, studies that use the concept of

---

[15] Kapoor, 2013

altruism as an explanatory of human behaviour are rare[16], a factor that indicates that the world of social marketing, NPOs and charity work in general is way more complex.

Many argue that altruism does not exist because humans want to gain something from what they do; hence it is always a situation of exchange. For instance, Baker et al explain that attempting to achieve something has been intrinsic to the human nature since its dawn[17]. Houston and Gassenheimer made similar affirmations earlier: in their view it is satisfying needs the real motivation to become involved in an exchange[18].

---

[16] Kapoor, 2013

[17] Baker et al. 2010

[18] Houston; Gassenheimer, 1987

Kotler too asserts that humans are indeed goal-seeking animals but he digs deeper. He underlines that people prefer some objectives to others and are able to anticipate the outcome of their actions, to drive their conducts and to create behaviours to gain their intended anticipated results[19]. Subsequently, the concept of exchange arises from this human continuous goal generation process and from an instinctive need to achieve such objectives.

Kotler defines marketing as "a social process by which individuals and groups obtain what they need and want through creating and exchanging products and value with others"[20]. From this statement it is possible to deduce that Kotler agrees with Houston and Gassenheimer as, in order to obtain what is

---

[19] Hastings; Domegan, 2013

[20] Kotler, 1967, Pg.4

needed, exchanges are not only inevitable but primordial.

In a more recent text, Kotler developed the five key prerequisites that in his view are essential for exchanges to take place:

1. at least two parties must participate;
2. each is capable of communication and delivery;
3. each is free to accept or reject the offer;
4. each believes it is appropriate/desirable to deal with the other;
5. both parties have something of value to the other[21].

In commercial marketing the presence of exchanges which satisfy Kotler's requirements is simple to spot.

---

[21] Kotler, 2000

Commercial marketers, such as myself, are driven by self-interest. After all, we are performing a paid job which involves convincing others that the use of the product/service we are selling is in their best interest. Moreover, customers too are driven by self-interest as they seek to satisfy their own needs and wants[22]. The exchange is, therefore, mutually beneficial, as marketers are rewarded with a salary and customers obtain what they desire.

However, the presence of exchanges in social marketing is more challenging to notice, as the benefits for social marketers are more ambiguous than the gains for commercial marketers.

As Bagozzi affirms, exchanges involve the transfer

---

[22] Hastings, 2007

of both tangible and intangible elements[23]. While commercial marketers participate in so-called *utilitarian exchanges,* which provide tangible products/services in return for an agreed amount of money, in social marketing we talk about a *symbolic exchange*, which is a mutual transfer of intangible elements[24]. Therefore, social marketers try to sell benefits that are not concrete and cannot be perceived, such as disease *prevention* or car accident *avoidance*[25]. This is indeed a challenge and definitely contributes to the ambiguity that surrounds social marketing.

Nevertheless, intangibility is not solely in social marketing: commercial marketing offers it too or at

---

[23] Bagozzi, 1979

[24] Bagozzi, 1975

[25] Hastings, 2007 and Bagozzi, 1975

least elements of it[26]. For instance, the tourism industry is mainly involved with selling experiences which are commercially marketed. Experiences are intangible and a basic example is dining out. Branding is a form of commercial marketing also based on intangibility. In fact, purchasing an item because of its brand indicates that the latter generates a positive reputation or a social symbol which leads people to select it. Have you ever spotted gals going to the extent of purchasing a fake Louis Vuitton purse just to be able to show the brand off to their peers? Or chaps wearing imitations of Rolex watches? So, social marketers are not the only ones to deal with intangibility as a challenge.

On one hand, 'though intangible, the benefits of

---

[26] Hastings, 2007 and Bagozzi, 1975

social marketing towards the society are significant. On the other hand, since they are mainly "probabilistic and inherently unattractive", they are often underestimated, leading to a lower value to be gained by social marketers compared to the advantages the targeted public obtains[27].

Such a limited gain is however only apparent, and there is a plethora of examples from the private sector which can prove it. Insurance companies, for instance, often release campaigns designed to limit car accidents. Their reduction, in fact, represents a concrete benefit for themselves who have to issue less monetary compensations to their clients[28]. Governments as well produce social marketing. Just think of the popular *SmokeFree* in the UK. Also

---

[27] Hastings, 2007, Pg.162

[28] Petzer et al, 2006

supported by the NHS, such a campaign seeks to diminish the national consumption of tobacco products. Hence, its aim is to benefit the society by raising an awareness of the health risks deriving from the use of this demerit good and to increase general disease avoidance amongst the citizens[29]. Again, a superficial eye could regard this campaign as the result of the *love* that a government can feel towards its population. Nevertheless, we know fairly well the situation differs drastically: significant and concrete advantages can be enjoyed by the releasers of this social marketing program. In fact, smoking provokes *negative externalities*.

Traditional economics teach us that negative externalities are costs that are consequential to an

---

[29] SmokeFree Resource Centre, n.d.

economic transaction. They emerge from either the production or consumption of a demerit good, which are potentially harmful to *third* parties[30]. They are external costs as they occur when the marginal social cost is higher than the marginal private cost. This is better depicted with a graphic representation:

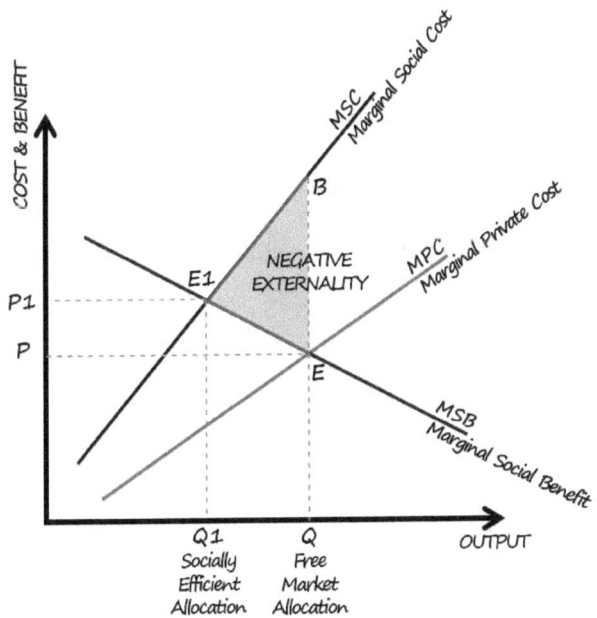

---

[30] Mankiw et al, 2013

As the graph illustrates, the socially efficient output would be at Q1, where the marginal social cost and benefit intersect (MSC = MSB), creating the equilibrium point E1. However, Q1 is at a lower output than the output engendered by the free market, which is at Q. In fact, the free market equilibrium is at point E. The negative externality exists when the marginal social cost of a particular economic activity is greater than the marginal social benefit. Any output between Q1 and Q creates a net welfare loss, thus a negative externality (area E,E1,B).

Tobacco is not deemed a demerit good because it harms smokers but because its consumption generates a social cost and undermines several third parties. An example is the NHS, which is supposedly condemned to a greater work load as more patients exist due to the diseases arising from smoking. Moreover, since the NHS is financed by the government, also the latter is impacted by the drawbacks of smoking.

Therefore, the production of social marketing campaigns against tobacco consumption not solely benefits the society, as it aims at preventing health problems in individuals, but also leads to important financial savings for the government.

The same reasoning applies when public institutions launch campaigns to promote the consumption of *merit goods*.

Following the World Health Organisation's recommendation in 2003, several countries initiated campaigns to encourage healthier nutritional habits.

After numerous such initiatives, the French government, for instance, mandated that any advertisement related to food and beverage must include one of the approved phrases promoting a balanced diet. Consequently, every French citizen has encountered countless times the stance "pour votre santé, mangez au moins cinq fruits et légumes par jour", translating to "for your health, consume at least five fruits and vegetables a day." France not only released its social campaigns but also forced the private sector to adopt them.

In contrast to demerit goods, which lead to negative externalities, merit goods generate positive externalities for third parties and occur when the marginal social benefit exceeds the marginal social cost.

Fruits and vegetables are classified as merit goods because they create positive externalities for groups unrelated to their production or consumption. In this scenario, the French government and the Social Security (Sécu) serve as examples of third parties benefiting from the campaign. It is not surprising that the initiative was spearheaded by these entities themselves.

Hence, the apparently intangible and small benefits that social marketers gain can actually be significant and concrete advantages.

On the one hand, it can be argued that social marketers working for social marketing agencies chose to embrace that career. Subsequently, if they did not care at all about the collective, they could have selected another paid occupation. This supports the existence of altruism as a human driving element.

On the other hand social marketing agencies are not common. Generally social marketing is produced either by commercial marketing agencies which are hired by businesses, NPOs and governmental organisations or directly by the latter themselves[31]. This signifies that the individuals behind social marketing campaigns do not produce solely these but focus also on other areas of marketing. As a result, they rarely choose to embrace a career in social marketing but just engage in it because the professional opportunity arises, a fact that supports the exchange theory.

---

[31] Lees-Marshment, 2014

Moreover, like commercial marketers, social marketers perform a job for which they obtain a concrete benefit: a wage. Hence, they do participate in exchanges and these are mutually beneficial.

Gillin and Schwartzman dare to argue that "companies actually have more to gain from social marketing than their consumer counterparts"[32]. In fact, while the target audience only gains awareness of a danger or a benefit, organisations that produce social marketing obtain financial rewards, sometimes even fiscal advantages and other benefits of different kinds pending on the sector in which they belong. This view implies that it is evident that altruism and philanthropy are not the factors that drive social marketers to help others, but

---

[32] Gillin; Schwartzman 2010, Pg.12

the gains that derive from such a work.

Resultantly, it is possible to deduce that there are no differences between commercial and social marketers intention-wise: "commercial marketers are not interested in satisfying consumer needs for the sake of it; they see this as the means to the end of profitability. By the same token, social marketers are not interested in educating people about health for the sake of it"[33].

Agreeing with Hastings' conclusion, Guy and Patton believe that altruism is not the reason that pushes people to turn the other cheek, not even in NPOs[34].

---

[33] Hastings, 2007, Pg. 44

[34] Guy; Patton, 1989

IT'S (NOT) THE THOUGHT THAT COUNTS

ANY VOLUNTEERS?

Some NPOs consist of paid employees, others are run by volunteers and the majority is formed by both[35]. Paid employees in NPOs do not differ from commercial and social marketers, as they obtain an evident reward. It is again a situation of exchange, where individuals in need get help while the helpers receive a salary.

---

[35] Moreland, 2006

This rationale, however, does not apply to volunteers who join NPOs. When discussing concepts like donation, charity, reward, philanthropy, we tend to automatically link them with money. However, money is neither the sole resource we can offer nor the most valuable one. What is the most precious asset we can own, give and receive? Time: for when you lose money, you can earn it again; but when you waste time, it is gone forever. Therefore, giving your time can be considered the most significant donation one can make.

Unlike paid employees, volunteers donate their time without monetary compensation, which leads us to the next main questions: why do they commit to a practice that does not enable them to make a living? If financial recompenses are not receivable, are volunteers truly altruistic?

In order to answer these, I thought about my own personal experiences. In fact, I have engaged in charity work since I was a sixth form student. The reason? Simple: it was a compulsory component of the International Baccalaureate (IB). Admittedly, that is why I did it, achieving the IB was not possible otherwise. Hence, in my case, I was definitely not being altruistic. Furthermore, charity work is encouraged by schools, such as mine, because it is an extra entry on relatively blank young CVs and in many countries, like the UK, a rather valued one. Yet, this is another example of exchange from which both the people in need and the helpers mutually benefit.

When I was eighteen, I volunteered in Thailand by joining an NPO. Although I performed a lot of charity work, I admit that initially I committed to it just because it was a different and cheaper way to visit another country. It was only when I was actually helping, that I felt a great sense of gratification as a result of the good I was doing. But in either moment was altruism the factor that led me to care about the others. There was always a benefit that I could enjoy behind my actions.

In 2016, I got involved in another volunteering organisation in Malaysia. I joined it as I needed to buy time to obtain a permanent work visa. Again, an exchange of benefits: my little students got their English lessons and I got a roof over my head and a daily meal for free for enough months for me to get my precious paper from the local government and start a new employed life as a marketer in Malaysia. That organisation, however, showed me an additional façade of the whole NPO business.

Funded mainly by considerably wealthy and extremely influential households in the Southeast Asian society, the NPO was a screen to display generosity and hide controversial political and financial manoeuvres. This not only showed a clear - and at this stage arguably balanced - exchange but also proved, at least to me, that sadly hypocrisy can indeed be a major component of NPOs.

As a result of these experiences, I do not believe that people who freely contribute in charity organisations and NPOs do it solely to benefit others. Just like in my recollections, there are advantages to be gained from volunteering. These can be divided into three main categories:

1. Concrete benefits
2. Psychological benefits
3. Social benefits

Examples of concrete benefits are tax deductions, admissions to special events[36], free meals, extra references in the CV, publicity, coverage of controversial actions.

The psychological benefits are more subjective. Some people may expect help from others in the future in return of their current contribution; others may feel empathy towards individuals in need and perhaps even guilt; many consider volunteering as an opportunity to help and subsequently satisfy their need to help and feel necessary: since such an opportunity may be considered as a relatively scarce commodity, it can represent a considerable value to acquire[37].

---

[36] Guy; Patton, 1989

[37] Guy; Patton, 1989

The social benefits include the need to adhere to social norms[38] and what are defined as *communal rewards,* such as the desire for social recognition, good reputation, wealth display, fame and respect[39]. These are very strong motivational elements. Mandeville had already understood it in the XVIII century in his Fable of the Bees, where he asserts the famous phrase: "pride and vanity have built more hospitals than all the virtues put together"[40].

Pending on individual perspectives, some motivators might be stronger than others. Guy and Patton believe that the most significant one is helping others only to obtain joy and pleasure in doing it. With this affirmation, the authors clearly mean that

---

[38] Guy; Patton, 1989

[39] Armstrong; Brown, 2009

[40] Mandeville, 1714, Pg. n/a

altruism does not exist as even performing a task for the pleasure of it leads to the attainment of something; thus it is an exchange of values[41]. The Dalai Lama XIV emphasised that altruism is the best source of happiness, and that happiness is not a pre-existing entity but rather a product of our own actions. This implies that happiness is not innate but rather a commodity to be attained. Recognizing happiness as an achievement suggests that striving for it can inspire motivation. Hence, engaging in actions that benefit others to obtain happiness represents a reciprocal exchange of values.

---

[41] Guy; Patton, 1989

IT'S (NOT) THE THOUGHT THAT COUNTS

WAR OR PEACE

So far we observed that views on the existence of altruism differ significantly and have generated endless debates.

Nevertheless, a prevailing stance among scholars in economics and business fields posits that the primary motivation for individuals to benefit others is rooted in the expectation of receiving something in return.

After a thorough reflection, I found myself more inclined to agree with the academics that dismiss altruism. Two reasons directed me towards this conclusion: one is the fact that the amount of scholars that support the exchange theory greatly outweighs the number of academics who consider altruism as a driving factor in human behaviour[42]; the second consists of my own personal experiences, such as volunteering in Asia and working as a commercial marketer in private companies, which push me to believe that the need to gain something in return plays a crucial role in humans' actions.

---

[42] Kapoor, 2013

Nevertheless, it would be rather shallow to stop here. The debate on the existence of altruism in business has haunted scholars for decades because it is a complex matter and it deserves a deeper reflection before a conclusion can be drawn.

In fact, there is one last main question that still needs an answer: are self-interest and altruism mutually exclusive?

IT'S (NOT) THE THOUGHT THAT COUNTS

SELFISH ALTRUISM

By dismissing altruism in favour of exchange, those academics imply that self-interest and altruism cannot coexist. How could they? Given that Compte defined altruism as the antonym of egoism, he left no room for compatibility.

Nevertheless, there are scholars, such as Andreasen, who envisage the possibility of a combination of the two antipodes, as several reasons can lead to the performance of an action[43]: "if a company has mixed motives", does the one that is perceived negatively suppress the positive[44]?

Let us clarify with an example: a government may want to release a campaign to promote an active life. Its reasons can be several: the reduction of the obesity rate, the prevention of illnesses, the avoidance of subsequent further costs to be incurred by public welfare. Whether one of these motives has weighted more than the others when deciding to release the campaign is something that cannot be known for sure - although we can make an educated guess...-. Furthermore, does the fact that one of these three reasons is to limit financial expenses

---

[43] Andreasen, 2001.

[44] Andreasen, 2001, Pg.6.

ruin the other two intentions?

The COVID-19 crisis provided compelling examples of the potential coexistence of altruism and self-interest. During the pandemic, numerous firms distributed freebies, Amazon Prime Video, Logitech, Ford Motor, Dyson to name a few. These acts raised questions about their underlying motives. Were they purely altruistic? On one hand, offering free items served as a demonstration of solidarity amid an unprecedented global crisis, while also keeping some employees engaged and compensated. On the other hand, it functioned as a strategy to garner positive publicity, reduce storage costs, or prevent the wastage of perishable goods.

Businesses that continued marketing efforts during the COVID-19 crisis exhibited a dual nature, being both self-interested and altruistic simultaneously. They pursued business activities to ensure survival while also contributing to the welfare of their workforce. By providing employment and laying the groundwork for future profits through promotional activities, these companies aimed to navigate through the crisis, enabling them to sustain salaries and fulfil tax obligations. The collective interest was vested in the survival and subsequent recovery of businesses, as it benefited not only the companies but also their labour and the broader economy.

Does the fact that some of the several reasons why these companies gave away products for free were to reduce financial losses annihilate the solidarity motive?

"If there are multiple motives, does it matter which

one dominates?"[45]. Andreasen believes not. Nonetheless, following his rationale, it is possible to discern that altruism is considered, rather than a reason for human behaviour, a consequence of it, whether intended or not. This forces us to reconsider entirely the angle from which we assess altruism.

Analysing Compte's statement, it is easy to notice that his words do not hint to whether altruism is a cause or a consequence. His is too vague of a definition and its incompleteness plays a pivotal role in this academic debate. Rather disappointing is the fact that the scholars quoted in this reflection do not seem to investigate much the origin of the term altruism. Definitions are wordy matters, not maths.

---

[45] Andreasen, 2001, Pg.6

They are assumptions, not axioms. Hence, they should be debated.

In this case the etymology of altruism is key in the argument. If we accept Compte's assertion without question, it is natural to agree with scholars like Baker et al. and Kotler, as whether a cause or a consequence, by definition altruism is not compatible with self-interest. And if there is a reward of any kind to be gained in all actions, it is always a matter of exchange and altruism is –yet another– mere form of idealism or utopian feature deriving from human hope and religion.

Yet, as aforementioned, Compte defined but did not invent from scratch the term. Like most vocabulary, altruism is the outcome of a linguistic evolutionary path which can be traced up to at least the ancient

Romans. *Alter,* the Latin root of altruism, is simply a nominative case meaning *the others* and implies neither a mutually exclusive relation nor a coexistence with another concept. If Compte's definition is ignored in favour of the more ancient origin of the word, then it is indeed possible to envisage a coexistence where self-interest does not preclude altruistic consequences, just like Andreasen believes. After all, our modern society and economy would not exist as we know them today if altruism and self-interest were mutually exclusive.

In fact, we can argue that making a choice driven by self-interest, such as selecting a career focused on profit generation, can be indeed considered altruistic as well. This is because, due to the way it has been organised, our modern society prospers from chain reaction based on consumption. For example, generating profit *self-interestingly* ignites a domino effect starting from the hiring of individuals, reducing costly unemployment, followed by the payment of wages which lead to an increase in entire households' purchase power that creates higher consumption levels which then raise revenues of other profit-generating parties, who can then reward their own labourers and so on till a rise in GDP occurs and the nation's economy grows. Concomitantly, salaries imply payable taxes which the government receives and can allocate in order to provide and/or improve welfare, public safety, social security, subsidies, etc. benefitting the society as a whole - whether governments do allocate honestly and intelligently those funds is an entirely different point.

Let us draw an example from a real world case study: the Bezos backlash. In September 2018 Amazon founder Jeff Bezos, one of the richest men in the world if not the wealthiest, announced that he would donate $2bn of his own wealth to finance a network of preschools and tackle homelessness in the States. Wow, this man is truly altruistic... Is he? Was he universally applauded? Nope. Instead, his pledge was bombarded by accusations of hypocrisy: in fact some undercover reporters exposed the modest wages of Amazon's employees which often did not suffice to cover rents, forcing them to sleep in tents outside of the company's infrastructures...[46] Several commented that it would have been more altruistic to use the money to raise salaries rather than donating it elsewhere, as paying a fair stipend

---

[46] BBC, 2018

to people who spend their life working for it is indeed as altruistic as giving it to charity. Of course, paying decent wages does not attract newspapers' headlines as much as big charity donations…

As we saw earlier, economic psychology attributes a narrower and more modern definition to altruism compared to Compte and explains it as the act of helping a party at your own expense. A self-interested profit-generator rewards its labour with his revenue; pays his taxes with his revenue; expands his employees' purchase power with his revenue. Hence the apparent egoistic profit-generator actually helps the collective socially and economically at his own cost by taking from his revenue. Does this not fit the definition economic psychology gives regarding altruism?

The foundation of our modern economy and society lies in the transformation of self-interest driven activities into benefits for the collective. Is this not a process that starts with egoism but ends with altruistic consequences? Does it not illustrate that self-interest and altruism can and are currently coexisting? Our modern society and economy would not exist the way we know them if it was not the case. Actually, one could argue that it is the combination of self-interest and altruism the key to achieving success in economic and business realms, today.

In these recent decades, society has become increasingly individualistic... rather flashy... perhaps vane... This trend has been significantly fuelled by the rise of social media. Whether we look at public personas, political figures or private citizens, all aspire to one thing: showing off to the biggest possible audience. And they want to portray themselves as what they wish to be perceived, not as to what they truly are. Welcome to the century of *selfish altruism*!

Selfish altruism refers to behaviours or actions that may outwardly appear altruistic, but are ultimately motivated by self-interest. In other words, individuals engaging in selfish altruism may perform actions that seem charitable or benevolent, but their underlying motive is to serve their own needs or desires, such as gaining social approval, recognition, or some form of personal satisfaction. Indeed, prominent displays of altruism are utilised as a means of portraying a crafted image of an individual or entity. As depicted by the aforementioned Jeff Bezos' case study, some might deem this phenomenon as hypocritical, but we will discuss this further in the next chapter.

What we can retain for now is that selfish altruism is a trend based on self-serving motives that engender altruistic actions. Thus, it implies that the coexistence of self-interest and altruism is a reality and that altruism exists but not as a driving element of a behaviour but rather as a consequence.

SHARING IS CARING

You, me... today we all are living the age of selfish altruism! Political rhetoric that appears ethical lacks substantial evidence and tangible support. Words that sound moral are disseminated through the media, yet they often hide naivety or even hypocrisy. Actions that appear generous serve as tools to build reputations and publicity campaigns.

We can all list dozens of stars, magnates and

politicians who are reported to have participated in substantial charity donations. Talk show mogul, Oprah Winfrey, made headlines in 2018 for a $2 million donation to the Smithsonian's National Museum of African American History and Culture. During the same year, the music industry power couple Beyoncé and Jay-Z, announced a $1 million scholarship program through their charitable foundation BeyGOOD. CEO of Tesla and SpaceX, Elon Musk, pledged $100 million to fund a prize for the best carbon capture technology in 2021. The list of examples could go on and on: whether it's Leonardo DiCaprio, Silvio Berlusconi, or Taylor Swift, hitting headlines with sizable contributions seems to represent the summit of success. If they have not made it up there yet, they have not become the star they wanted to be. Once they have reached that pinnacle, that's when Wikipedia starts listing them as *philanthropists* and, of course, tabloids go wild: the bigger the donation, the bigger the visibility, thus the bigger the success. And it becomes a contest of who pees the furthest!

Moreover, their actions are driven not only by a desire for publicity but also by the intention to boost sales. Making substantial donations to charity is frequently viewed as an investment, as it can influence consumer behaviour. For instance, it is proven that individuals are more likely to buy a product or service if it is associated with charitable giving. And there are, of course, instances of unethical behaviours, such as the recent controversy involving Chiara Ferragni, an Italian influencer, who was recently accused of deceiving the public with her involvement in a charity campaign linked to a pink Christmas pandoro.

On a broader scale, some of the world's wealthiest families have forged enduring legacies primarily through their philanthropic endeavours rather than through their actual business ventures. Notable examples include renowned houses such as the Rockefellers, the Peabodys, the Rothschilds, the Gates, the Windsors, the Sacklers, to name a few.

On the other hand, while it is true that often their reasons are to attract good publicity, make up for scandals, enhance their reputation, increase revenues and that these are indeed social rewards received in exchange for their donations, it is equally crucial to consider the recipients of such largesse. When these contributions are directed toward socially beneficial causes and projects in a transparent and accountable manner, their impact can be immensely valuable, leading to positive changes in the world that can endure for generations. King Hussein of Jordan, for instance, was reported to have sold one of his London houses to gather the necessary funds and renovate the Dome of the Rock Cupola in Jerusalem with a 24-carat golden covering. Naturally this act garnered a lot of media attention but also contributed to preserve an icon of cultural, religious and artistic heritage.

Moreover, wealthy celebrities *choose* to allocate their own funds to support social causes. This decision is not coerced, nor is it legally mandated. It is a voluntary choice they make. So, 'though they engage in exchanges driven by self-interest, are they not sacrificing significant portions of their own wealth for the benefit of society? Do these practices not coincide with the economic definition of altruism? Do they not yield altruistic outcomes?

The Bible's New Testament contains a story that resonates very well with this topic. It is called the *Widow's Offering*:

> [41] *Jesus sat down opposite the place where the offerings were put and watched the crowd putting their money into the temple treasury. Many rich people threw in large amounts.*
>
> [42] *But a poor widow came and put in two very small copper coins, worth only a few cents.*
>
> [43] *Calling his disciples to him, Jesus said, "Truly I tell you, this poor widow has put more into the treasury than all the others.*

⁴⁴ They all gave out of their wealth; but she, out of her poverty, put in everything — all she had to live on."

(Mark 12:41-44)

In this tale the poor widow, who gives all her meagre possessions away, is praised while the rich who donated only part of their wealth but in larger amounts are despised. Earlier, we learnt that the purpose of altruistic behaviours is to benefit others, even when these damage the actor (Monroe, 1996). The widow can, hence, be considered altruistic. *It is the thought that counts!* we all said once at least. But concretely, the world does not run on mere thoughts. Hell might be paved by good intentions but stomachs are not. The poor lady surely made a greater sacrifice donating all her cents but the temple would hardly stand if it had no wealthy donors. By the same token, a lot of charities, social causes, green initiatives and cultural foundations would hardly go on if wealthy personas did not donate conspicuous amounts. After all, they are the ones who can afford to give away enough to make a real difference to the causes they support.

Moreover, offering all her coins does not prove the widow's altruistic nature. Consciously or not, she too may have envisaged a gain in return, such as divine pardon, certain passage to Heaven or other psychological and social rewards.

Moreover, the widow finds herself with nothing left, prompting questions about how she plans to move forward and sustain herself. Despite her initial altruistic act of donating all her possessions, she now faces a situation where she needs assistance.

If we transpose this biblical narrative into a modern developed country, the widow who gave away all her coins now depends more significantly on public welfare than when she possessed them. While her complete donation might have been driven by altruistic intentions, it actually transforms her into a greater societal burden, becoming, in economic terms, an increase in the nation's deadweight: supporting her now is more expensive than before her charitable gesture. Afterall, in our society, we may not all be producers but we are all consumers.

Drawing parallels between the destitute widow and unpaid volunteers in non-profit organisations, it becomes apparent that, unless volunteers sustain their period of service with pre-existing income or passive earnings from sources other than the NPO, they, too, can become an economic burden on society. And who foots the bill for these burdens? Well, it is us, the regular folks, the income-generating and tax-paying citizens of the country. The collective bears the brunt of this increased expense, since welfare relies on funding from profit generators along with individuals akin to the wealthy figures in the Biblical tale. These individuals contribute only a portion of their possessions, ensuring substantial resources are available to society while maintaining enough for their own survival without becoming a burden to the collective. Society benefits form profit-generators not from income-less parties. So, how can profit-makers gat tagged as villains in this altruism debacle? And how can it be asserted that self-interest and altruism are not compatible?

The widow's total giveaway might have been intentionally altruistic but ends up being the opposite in its consequences. Conversely, those who contributed only a portion of their possessions, despite facing diminished regard from the Bible's perspective, engendered the greatest benefits, as their donation did not create a heightened need for assistance.

In contrast to this parable, let us turn to a teaching from Buddha: *a candle can light thousands of candles without extinguishing itself*. This proverb emphasises the importance of self-sustenance over self-sacrifice: sharing is caring, self-sacrifice is not. In case of a loss of pressure on an airplane, we are advised to secure our own oxygen masks before even assisting our own children. The underlying principle is clear – one must prioritise self-help to be capable of helping others effectively. If you are not receiving enough sustenance, you are not in a position to provide it to others. You simply cannot pour from an empty cup. Without accruing wealth self-interestingly, how can anyone engage in altruistic donations to benefit others?

Neoclassical economics lies on the premise that individuals aim at maximizing utility, whether defined as income, wealth, or profit[47]. Within this framework of individual optimization, people make choices by selecting the most favourable opportunity from a set of permissible options[48]. Consequently, those who willingly put themselves at a disadvantage to benefit others do not prosper. Hence, from the neo-classical

---

[47] Simon, 1991

[48] Arnsperger, 2000

standpoint, altruism in economic contexts is incompatible with rational decision-making: in economic settings altruism/charity just should not exist.

THE THOUGHTS THAT DO COUNT

Whether a mere fantasy or a tangible reality, Comte's definition provides a foundational entry point for grappling with the concept of altruism.

However, his definition is simplistic and superficial and, consequently, numerous alternatives have emerged, varying based on the author's opinion and the specific field within which they operate.

Nonetheless, they all lie on the basis that altruism is a behaviour consisting in generating positive outcomes to others, at the actor's own expenses and, most importantly, without expecting something in return. The latter point is the reason why, as we saw throughout this text, perspectives on the very existence of altruism spark ongoing debates.

In economics and business related fields, the majority of scholars believe that the real motivation of humans to benefit others is the need to gain something in return. Some, like Baker et al and Kotler, justify such a behaviour by affirming that it is beyond human control because it constitutes a fundamental aspect of our species[49]. Others, like Guy and Patton, argue that altruism does not even

---

[49] Baker et al, 2010 and Hastings; Domegan, 2013

exist[50].

Whether intentional, sought after, requested or unconsciously wanted, I believe that every action stems from an inherent expectation of acquiring something in return, be it in the form of tangible, social, or psychological benefits. Happiness, pleasure and personal fulfilment stand out as potent motivators indeed and do constitute concrete rewards for one's actions: non-profit organisations, social marketers and even volunteers have something to gain form their activities. Hence, all actions are a matter of exchange of values.

However, I reckon altruism *can* exist, yet not as an explanatory for human behaviour but rather as a

---

[50] Guy; Patton, 1989

consequence. As we reviewed earlier, neo-classical economics asserts that altruism clashes with rational decision-making, suggesting that it should not even have a place in economic settings. Personally, I find this stance quite an overstatement. Financial donations and volunteer time, through charities and NPOs for instance, enable the functioning of some essential services, support research and address social challenges. Dismissing them completely would jeopardise societal well-being.

However, if altruism is engendered by a total self-sacrifice, then the neoclassical statement makes a valid point. As we discussed through the *Widow's Offering* tale, giving away all our wealth or dedicating all our time without economic compensation is detrimental not only to ourselves but also to society. Given the way our modern economy is structured, individual financial strain leads inevitably to a collective economic burden. Thus, self-sacrifice is not altruistic, it is irrational and perhaps just vane. Worse: it winds up being actually selfish.

Conversely, a self-interested profit seeker who complies with the law, produces honest goods/services, ensures fair compensation for employees, and fulfils tax obligations can stimulate far more substantial economic growth and contribute to overall societal progress. On a practical level, it is fundamental for both Individuals and businesses to balance altruistic efforts with financial responsibilities and to consider the broader impact of their actions in order to make *sustainable* contributions to society. Only responsible giving and strategic philanthropy can contribute to both personal well-being and positive societal outcomes.

In essence, I believe that self-interest benefits the collective, so it engenders altruistic consequences. Hence, self-interest and altruism *can* coexist.

Moreover, self-interest and altruism *do* coexist: in today's era of selfish altruism, integrating both is crucial for attaining success in business. People seek visibility and want to showcase themselves as what they wish to be perceived by others, rather than as their true selves. Prominent displays of altruism are indeed utilised as a means to gain. Hence, selfish altruism is motivated by the desire to obtain something. Its foundation lies on self-interested motives which foster a system of exchanges that create altruistic consequences.

Some may contend that this phenomenon borders on hypocrisy. Nevertheless, if the phenomenon of selfish altruism motivates individuals to engage in beneficial actions, does it truly matter if their underlying motives are not as noble and selfless as they present them to be? Some scholars, such as Andreasen, think not and neither do I. The significance of intentions is a spiritual concern, the judgment of which I leave to individuals' conscience. As a businesswoman, I focus on evaluating the concrete consequences of actions. Selfish altruism is acceptable in my view if it leads to positive outcomes both on an individual and collective level. For example, I am convinced that the dual benefit derived from social marketing and non-profit organisations, benefiting both society and themselves, renders these practices even more valuable than purely altruistic gestures. When these efforts yield advantages for both parties, more individuals reap the benefits, amplifying the overall impact and creating a win-win scenario.

My point of view is inspired by the *greatest happiness* principle: a utilitarian approach fathered by John Stuart Mill which is calculative and consequentialist in its essence and emphasises on collective utility. In a nutshell, it focuses on the outcome of an action rather than its nature[51][52]. In my opinion, the reception of rewards, whether in the form of a salary or social and psychological gratifications, in return for helping others, creates

---

[51] Mill, 1870

[52] I started this reflection by criticising Auguste Compte and his vague definition of altruism to then conclude it by taking refuge in John Stuart Mill's utilitarianism. It is important to note, however, that Mill's work was highly influenced by Compte. In fact, the two men were engaged in a pen-friendship for most of their lives.

exchanges that are inherently positive and pivotal for both individuals and the society as a whole.

Ultimately, our modern society is an interconnected network encompassing governments, populations, foundations, organisations, associations, enterprises and so on. It is a gargantuan web. Therefore, exchanges can even be deemed superior to acts stemming purely from altruism, if it actually exists, as they have the potential to benefit the greatest number of people by leveraging the interconnectedness of our society.

Anticipating potential counterarguments to my conclusions, I shall end this reflection by invoking the well-known Machiavellian thought: *the end justifies the means.*

IT'S (NOT) THE THOUGHT THAT COUNTS

BIBLIOGRAPHY

Andreasen, A. R. (2001), Ethics in Social Marketing, Georgetown University Press

Andreasen, A.R. (2003), The Life Trajectory of Social Marketing – Some Implications, Marketing Theory, 3(3), 293—303

Armstrong, M. Brown, D. (2009), Strategic Reward: Implementing More Effective Reward Management, Kogan Page

Arnsperger, C. (2000). Methodological Altruism as an Alternative Foundation for Individual Optimization. Ethical Theory and Moral Practice, 3(2), 115–136.

Baker, M.J. , Baker, M. John, Saren, M. (2010), Marketing Theory: A Student Text, SAGE

BBC. (2018), The Bezos Backlash: Is 'big philanthropy' a charade?, Retrieved from: www.bbc.com/news/business-45520594 (Accessed: 04/06/2019)

Bagozzi, R.P. (1975), Marketing and Exchange, Journal of Marketing, Vol.39, 32-39

Bagozzi, R.P. (1979), Toward a Formal Theory of Marketing Exchange, in Conceptual and Theoretical Developments in Marketing, Brown, S. Lamb, C., eds., Chicago: American Marketing association, 431-447

Ben-Ner, A. Jones, D. (1995) Employee Participation, Ownership and Productivity: A Theoretical Framework. Industrial Relations, 34(4), 532-554

Cicloni, F. (1825), A Grammar of the Italian Language, London: John Murray

Compte, A. Congrev, R.(tr.). (1891), The Catechism of Positive Religion, London: John Chapman

Gillin, P. Schwartzman, E. 2010, Social Marketing to the Business Customer: Listen to Your B2B Market, Generate Major Account Leads, and Build Client Relationships, John Wiley & Sons

Guy, B.S. Patton, W.E. (1989), The Marketing of Altruistic Causes: Understanding Why People Help, The Journal of Consumer Marketing, Vol.6, No.1, Emerald Publishing Ltd

Hastings, G. 2007, Social Marketing: Why Should the Devil Have All the Best Tunes?, Butterworth-Heinemann

Hastings, G. Domegan, C. (2013), Social Marketing: From Tunes to Symphonies, Routledge

Houston F.S. Gassenheimer J.B. (1987), Marketing and Exchange, The Journal of Marketing, 3-18

Kapoor, A. (2013), Dynamics of Competitive Advantage and Consumer Perception in Social Marketing, IGI Global

Kotler, P. (1967), Marketing Management: Analysis, Planning, and Control, Prentice-Hall.

Kotler, P. (2000), Marketing management, Prentice Hall of India

Kotler, P. Zaltman, G. (1971), Social marketing: an Apporach to Planned Social Change, Journal of Marketing, Vol.35, 3-12

Lees-Marshment, J. (2014), Political Marketing: Principles and Application, Routledge

MacFadyen, L. Stead, M. Hastings G. (1999), A Synopsis of Social Marketing, Retrieved from: www.evidenceintopractice.scot.nhs.uk/media/135280/social_marketing_synopsis.pdf (Accessed: 18/03/2015)

Mandeville, B., The Fable of the Bees or Private Vices, Publick Benefits, 2 vols. With a Commentary Critical, Historical, and Explanatory by F.B. Kaye (Indianapolis: Liberty Fund, 1988). Vol. 1. Retrieved 4/18/2015 from the World Wide Web: http://oll.libertyfund.org/titles/846

Mankiw, N.G. Taylor, M.P. Ashwin, A. (2013), Business Economics, Cengage Learning EMEA

Mill, J.S. (1870), Utilitarianism, Longmans Green

Monroe, KR. (1996), Heart of altruism: perceptions of a common humanity. Ewing, NJ, USA: Princeton University Press

Moreland, J. (2008). Charities that Charge: A Communicative Investigation into the Social Entrepreneurial Nonprofit, ProQuest

Perfect Circle, (n.d), Official Website. Retrieved from: perfect-circle.co.uk/ (Accessed: 15/04/2015)

Petzer, D. Ismail, Z. Roberts-Lombard, M. Hern, L. Klopper, H. Subramani, D. Wakeham, M. Chipp, K. Berndt, A. (2006), Fresh Perspectives: Marketing, Pearson South Africa

Powell, W.W. Steinberg, R. (2006), The Nonprofit Sector: A Research Handbook, Yale University Press

Simon, Herbert A. 1991. "Organizations and Markets." Journal of Economic Perspectives, 5 (2): 25-44. DOI: 10.1257/jep.5.2.25

SmokeFree Resource Centre, (n.d.). Official Website. Retreived from: resources.smokefree.nhs.uk/ (Accessed: 17/04/2015)

Zunz, O. (2012), Philanthropy in America: A History. Princeton, NJ: Princeton University Press

IT'S (NOT) THE THOUGHT THAT COUNTS

ABOUT THE AUTHOR

Victoria Schaal is a Franco-Italian, but British-educated businesswoman who blends revenue acquisition expertise with creative skills to optimise business profitability.

Originally from Paris, France, Victoria Schaal's upbringing primarily took place in Venice, Italy, and the UK, where she earned a degree with honours in business management and marketing with advanced proficiency in Spanish from the University of Exeter.

Her professional journey has been a dynamic fusion of business expertise, primarily focused on revenue acquisition strategies, and creative pursuits, especially in photography and graphic design.

Throughout her career, she has embraced the nomadic lifestyle of a serial expatriate, living and working across Europe, Southeast Asia, Central America, West Africa, and the Middle East.

Today, Victoria lives in Oman. Her professional focus centres on fostering business growth through revenue acquisition and management plans, business development, pricing strategies, and sales and marketing enhancement. She seamlessly integrates her business acumen and particularly her marketing skills with commercial photography and graphic design to offer comprehensive solutions to her clients and partners which operate in various industries and countries. She was elected "Most trailblazing business leader of the year 2024" by CIO Today Magazine.

In 2019, Victoria published her dissertation "How do you like it? Customer services: Personalization or Standardization," which analyses the efficiency of major approaches to consumer support. It is available on Amazon worldwide.

Her passion for visual arts has also garnered recognition on global platforms: she was selected as a "Leader in Contemporary Art 2020" by Capsules Australia and included in their eponymous volume; she was listed as one of the "100 Best Photographers 2021" by Photographize Magazine New York and featured in their annual tome; a number of her artistic pieces have been showcased in esteemed media outlets such as BBC News, Fraction Mag, and Artist CloseUp; some of her best artworks are exhibited at the Saatchi Art Gallery.

2021 marked the release of Victoria's debut photobook "Venetian Visions," which features experimental photographs of her beloved hometown. It is available on Amazon and Blurb worldwide in Italian and English.

Victoria Schaal is reachable on LinkedIn and via email: vs@victoriaschaal.com
www.victoriaschaal.com

IT'S (NOT) THE THOUGHT THAT COUNTS

BY THE SAME AUTHOR:

VICTORIA SCHAAL

NEW EDITION

HOW DO YOU LIKE IT?

CUSTOMER SERVICES: STANDARDISATION OR PERSONALISATION

INTRODUCTION

'The customer is king' affirmed Mahatma Ghandi and today its truth is widely recognised (Kotler et al, 2009). Customers represent the fuel of businesses and are the nucleus around which the discipline of marketing revolves (Fogli, 2006; Deming, 1986; Peppers and Rogers, 2005).

However, classical marketing theory has prioritised the acquisition of new customers over their retention, a topic which has been erroneously neglected for long (Kotler et al, 2009).

Nonetheless, times have changed and both academics and companies are adapting to the novelties. Technological advancements, easily and rapidly accessible information, consumer-driven legislation and a higher level of competition in the worldwide market have led to the so called customer empowerment. Customers, in fact, have now a broader range of purchase choices and can refer to a variety of different sources of information before making their final decisions (Cook, 2010, Kotler et al, 2009; Prahald and Ramswamy, 2004).

Thus, nowadays customers have become businesses' primary concern: from being predominantly product-centric, firms now tend to implement consumer-oriented strategies (Tiu Wright et al, 2006).

Retaining existing customers is just as important as acquiring new ones. It enables a business to keep competitors at arm's length, provides the grounds for long-term profitability, increases the customer base of a firm, ensuring a valuable asset, and is believed to be economical compared to seeking new customers (Kotler et al, 2009; Reinartz et al, 2005; Levitt, 1983; Fornell and Wernerfelt, 1987; Oliver, 1999).

According to several, the key to customer retention is the construction of solid long-term relationships between business and clientele. The creation of customer loyalty, the enhancement of consumer satisfaction and the increase in customer-perceived value all play a fundamental role in the generation of a robust seller-buyer bond (Gronroos, 2000; Schieffer, 2005; Kotler et al, 2009; Lovelock and Wirtz, 2004). Nevertheless, the bridge that strengthens it is the customer services department, which represents the key to the achievement of the aforementioned goals (Fogli, 2006).

Customer services are increasingly gaining more importance in entities all around the world. Over the past few decades attention to this sector from both businesses and scholars has significantly risen and studies and journal papers have spawned in academia (Schneider and White, 2004; Fogli, 2006).

The delivery of customer services is perhaps

one of the most explored aspects of the topic (Schneider and White, 2004). Nonetheless, it is rather ample, multifaceted and mined by disagreements. The approach that should be undertaken by agents when interacting with customers is an area of service delivery still dominated by on-going debates. In fact, scholars present two distinct approaches that can be applied to communications: while one recommends the customisation of service according to the personal features of consumers, the other supports standardising interactions implying that every customer should be treated with the same high standards.

Although plenty has been written concerning this argument, the literature has failed to reach consensus. Generally, scholars tend to debate about the benefits and drawbacks of each approach, considering aspects like time and financial efficiency. However, their conclusions follow logical rationales based solely on theoretical material. None seems to have approached the question by also collecting primary data, such as by gathering information directly from consumers in order to understand what people favour when dealing with customer services.

The innovative aspect of this research lies in the inclusion of not solely a thorough review of theory but also direct enquiries to people in order to provide a balanced final judgment on which a conclusion can be drawn.

Researching this area not solely adds up to the

existing studies about customer services and their delivery, but also contributes to the reaching of a reliable and applicable result, which scholars have not produced yet.

Several businesses nowadays invest large funds on the training of their customer services and on quality checks of their deliveries. Determining whether a best method of delivering customer services exists provides firms, especially new-born and small ones, extra knowledge on which they may base their training programs without having to seek the assistance of costly third parties.

Thus, the objectives of this study are:
a) to explore how individuals prefer customer services to be delivered and

b) to determine which approach –customisation or standardisation- is more effective at retaining customers.

Available now on Amazon worldwide

IT'S (NOT) THE THOUGHT THAT COUNTS

IT'S (NOT) THE THOUGHT THAT COUNTS

www.ingramcontent.com/pod-product-compliance
Lightning Source LLC
Chambersburg PA
CBHW070150230526
45471CB00002B/594